T0058013

60

FARRAR
STRAUS
GIROUX

ALSO BY THOM GUNN

Fighting Terms

The Sense of Movement

Poems 1950–1966:
A Selection (with Ted Hughes)

Positives (with Ander Gunn)

Touch

Moly and *My Sad Captains*

Jack Straw's Castle

Selected Poems 1950–1975

The Occasions of Poetry:
Essays in Criticism and Autobiography

The Passages of Joy

Shelf Life

Collected Poems

Boss Cupid

The Man with
Night Sweats

The Man with
Night Sweats

THOM GUNN

Farrar Straus Giroux

New York

Farrar, Straus and Giroux
18 West 18th Street, New York 10011

Copyright © 1992 by Thom Gunn
Introduction copyright © 2007 by August Kleinzahler
All rights reserved
Printed in the United States of America
Originally published in 1992 by Faber and Faber Limited,
Great Britain
Published in 1992 in the United States by Farrar, Straus and Giroux
This paperback edition, 2007

Library of Congress Control Number: 2006940797
ISBN-13: 978-0-374-53068-6
ISBN-10: 0-374-53068-8

www.fsgbooks.com

P1

Contents

Introduction by August Kleinzahler vii

1
The Hug   3
To a Friend in Time of Trouble   4
Bone   6
An Invitation   7
The Differences   9
Lines for My 55th Birthday   11
Philemon and Baucis   12
Odysseus on Hermes   13
Seesaw   15

2
A Sketch of the Great Dejection   19

3
Patch Work   23
The Life of the Otter   25
Three for Children   27
Skateboard   29
Well Dennis O'Grady   30
Outside the Diner   31
Improvisation   33
Old Meg   34
Yellow Pitcher Plant   35
Tenderloin   37
Looks   39

To Isherwood Dying   41
The Stealer   42
JVC   44
Barren Leaves   45
Jamesian   46
Meat   47
Cafeteria in Boston   48
Nasturtium   50
The Beautician   51
'All Do Not All Things Well'   52

4
The Man with Night Sweats   57
In Time of Plague   59
Lament   61
Terminal   65
Still Life   66
The Reassurance   67
Words for Some Ash   68
Sacred Heart   69
Her Pet   71
Courtesies of the Interregnum   73
To the Dead Owner of a Gym   75
Memory Unsettled   76
The J Car   77
To a Dead Graduate Student   79
The Missing   80
Death's Door   82
A Blank   84

Acknowledgements and Notes   87

Introduction

by August Kleinzahler

On a January evening in 1983, Andrew Moss, a professor of epidemiology at the University of California, San Francisco, spoke to a gathering of the Alice B. Toklas Democratic Club. The venue was an upstairs room at the Café du Nord, a music club on the fringes of the Castro district, the largest predominantly gay neighborhood in San Francisco.

Moss, an expat Londoner who was one of the pioneers in AIDS research, told the assembled that there was a worrying disease turning up among gay men that behaved like a contagious cancer, in many instances a rare cancer called Kaposi's sarcoma, and that brought along with it a number of opportunistic infections, including Pneumocystis carinii. HIV itself hadn't been identified quite yet, but since 1981, initial descriptions of immunodeficiency symptoms in very sexually active young gay men had been appearing in medical journals and the press.

Moss went on to explain that one in 300 gay men already had the disease, believing privately at the time that the estimated rate of infection was closer to 20–30 percent. In fact, estimates of 45 percent began to be released as soon as the end of 1984, after serological tests became available earlier that year. At the time of Moss's talk there was something on the order of 50,000 gay men living in San Francisco. Fifteen years later, in 1998, the city would have experienced 21,000 AIDS-related deaths in the period.

In the spring of 1993, Moss, who is that rare combination of scientist and litterateur, reviewed Thom Gunn's *The Man with Night Sweats* in the *Hungry Mind Review*. Moss praised, among many other qualities, the way the "calm and formality" of Gunn's style served to contain his horror at the daily processes of a man's dying from AIDS pneumonia. Moss here was writing about the poem "Lament," which he had heard Gunn read aloud at a poetry reading in the mid-1980s:

> . . . Nothing remained
> But death by drowning on an island sea
> of your own fluids, which it seemed could be
> Kindly forestalled by drugs. Both could and would:
> Nothing was said, everything understood,
> At least by us . . .

"Lament" is one of seventeen poems that make up the fourth and final section of *The Man with Night Sweats*. It is one of Gunn's longest poems – 117 lines – and written in rhyming couplets. All but two of the poems in this last section are written in meter and rhyme, and all but one, "Her Pet" (about Germain Pilon's tomb carving for Valentine Balbiani), on the subject of AIDS. It was the poet's custom, when writing on subjects that challenged his emotional equilibrium, to contain the material through meter and rhyme.

The subject of "Lament" was a man named Allan Noseworthy, a close friend of Gunn's and the household he shared with several other gay men, including the great love of his youth and his lifelong companion, Mike Kitay. Noseworthy died in 1986 of AIDS.

By the time of Moss's address to the Alice B. Toklas Club in 1983, Gunn, like most gay men at the time, would have been aware of the early reports of a new disease affecting homosexual men but probably would not have given it too much attention. Gunn's *The Passages of Joy* had been published the year before, in 1982. Although the book received relatively little attention critically, it was Gunn's first collection in which he had fully come out of the closet, at least for anyone awake to see. He'd hinted at his homosexuality in *Jack Straw's Castle* (1976), and his work had appeared in a gay anthology called *The Male Muse* (1973). Gunn would have been pleased to come out earlier, but that would have jeopardized his residency status in the United States, where he'd been living since 1954 (though he never did apply for U.S. citizenship).

But if Gunn hadn't been paying much attention to the new disease, this disinterest was to change dramatically as his friend Noseworthy quickly deteriorated before his eyes. What had been an abstraction only a few months before was now a full-blown nightmare, nothing less than a plague among sexually active gay men, of whom Thom Gunn was very much one: a regular in the gay bars and bathhouses south of Market Street, a wonderfully handsome and charming man with large appetites.

Thom Gunn was in his fifties when he wrote *The Man with Night Sweats*, and in full command of his mature style, which began to take shape in the second part of his collection *My Sad Captains* (1961) and became fully realized in *Moly* (1971). From 1961 on, Gunn moved back and forth between free verse and closed forms, not according to an overarching scheme but as the material at hand recommended. His subject was the city, and he wrote of how character and event were played out on its street corners, in bars, bathhouses, taxis, and stairwells. Baudelaire's "Tableaux parisiens" from *Les Fleurs du mal* were as important to him as any poetry written in English, for San Francisco was for Gunn what Paris was for Baudelaire. The poetry cannot be separated from the place, by design.

The other central component of his mature poetry is its voice, which is highly unusual for a poet writing in the second half of the twentieth century. Gunn early on came under the influence of the Elizabethan poets Shakespeare, Donne, and Jonson, in which there's no identifiable personality to the "I," the voice in the poetry. Even in the most intimate of poems, the voice is detached, impersonal. On top of this, Gunn favors what is called the plain style, a taste he picked up from one of his mentors, Yvor Winters. One of its chief exemplars is Ben Jonson, a poet Gunn valued very highly and, to an extent, modeled his own work on. The plain style is just that: clear in diction and movement, devoid of rhetoric and poetic figures, inclining toward the way people speak without sounding colloquial. Gunn's fascination with the city as a backdrop for character and event, along with his anachronistically distanced, rather neutral voice, turned out to be the perfect mix for his poetic witnessing of the plague he was soon to find himself in the midst of.

Gunn has a well-known essay on the poetry of Ben Jonson in which he defends Jonson against the claim that he writes "occasional" poetry. "All poetry is occasional," Gunn writes, "whether the occasion is an external event like a birthday or a declaration of war, whether it is an occasion of the imagination, or whether it is in some sort of combination of the two."* Gunn goes on to explain that it is the job of the poet to "stay true" to that occasion. "The truer he is to it, the closer he sticks to what for him is its authenticity, the more he will be able to draw from it in the adventures that it produces, adventures that consist of the experience of writing."

Clive Wilmer discusses this notion in his introduction to Gunn's book of essays *The Occasions of Poetry*, writing, "The first loyalty of writers like Jonson who are 'true to their occasions' must be not to the self, nor to some prior ideology or faith, nor even to the imagination, but to the facts of experience." Wilmer goes on to quote from another Gunn essay in the collection, this one about William Carlos Williams. In that essay Gunn writes of Williams's "habitual sympathy, by which he recognizes his own energy" in that of other lives. The last sentence of the Williams essay reads: "For it is a humane action to attempt the rendering of a thing, person, or experience in the exact terms of its existence."

AIDS is the great occasion of *The Man with Night Sweats*, to be sure, but if it is the central occasion of the book, it is not the only occasion. It is easy to forget that the seventeen poems that constitute part 4 of the collection make up a little less than half of the book. Some of Gunn's finest poems here are not about AIDS at all, in-

---

*Thom Gunn, *The Occasions of Poetry: Essays in Criticism and Autobiography* (Berkeley, Calif.: North Point Press, 1982).

cluding two stunning poems that begin the book, "The Hug" and "To a Friend in Time of Trouble," both addressed to Mike Kitay, the occasion of the first:

> I dozed, I slept. My sleep broke on a hug,
> Suddenly, from behind,
> In which the full lengths of our bodies pressed:
> Your instep to my heel,
> My shoulder-blades against your chest.
> It was not sex, but I could feel
> The whole strength of your body set,
> Or braced, to mine,
> And locking me to you
> As if we were still twenty-two
> When our grand passion had not yet
> Become familial.
> My quick sleep had deleted all
> Of intervening time and place.
> I only knew
> The stay of your secure firm dry embrace.

Gunn would not have known, when he wrote this poem, what losses from AIDS lay not far ahead of him. But this poem gains particular resonance when read in the context of what was to follow. Kitay, like Gunn, was to survive the crisis, and the two lived together until Gunn's death in April 2004.

There are dazzling poems throughout the first three sections: epigrams; elegies to J. V. Cunningham and Christopher Isherwood; poems written for children; observations from nature; a poem about an otter Gunn sees at the Desert Museum in Tucson; another poem about nasturtium, a plant that seems to thrive everywhere in San Francisco ("A golden runaway / Still running, strewing gold"); yet another about a yellow pitcher plant; an extraordinary poem entitled "Patch Work" about the mockingbird. And a poem about a lover that ends:

> But think back on that night in January,
> When casually distinct we shared the most
> And lay upon a bed of clarity
> In luminous half-sleep where the will was lost.
> We woke at times and as the night got colder
> Exchanged a word, or pulled the clothes again
> To cover up the other's exposed shoulder,
> Falling asleep to the small talk of the rain.

Eros was the primary generative and organizing principle in Thom Gunn's adult life. I don't think it's any more evident in his own body of work than it is in that of many other poets; perhaps it's less evident. This may be because the nature of his sexuality could not safely be engaged in his poetry, at least directly, until relatively late in his writing life. But in his broader life, sexual love, infatuation, whatever one likes to call it, consumed this particular poet, if not to a unique degree then to a very profound degree. That Eros' dark complement, Thanatos, should present itself so dramatically at this point in the poet's life, and in the guise of a sexually transmitted fatal disease, provided the extraordinary occasion of the AIDS-related poems of part 4 in *The Man with Night Sweats*. Gunn treats this exact subject in his poem "In Time of Plague":

My thoughts are crowded with death
and its draws so oddly on the sexual
that I am confused
confused to be attracted
by, in effect, my own annihilation.
Who are these two, these fiercely attractive men
who want me to stick their needle in my arm?

The poem continues with the poet questioning his own
desire for a reckless tryst, deciding finally:

I weigh possibilities
till I am afraid of the strength
of my own health
and of their evident health.

The two "get restless at last with my indecisiveness"
and head off into "the moving concourse of people,"

carrying in their faces and throughout their bodies
the news of life and death.

After the death of Allan Noseworthy came the del-
uge. Gunn, like many gay men of the era, lost not some
but most of his friends. The dying was at its worst in
the late eighties. Gunn would, at one point, lose four
close friends in one month. In "Death's Door," a poem
of consolation, he imagines these friends in the afterlife:

After their processing, the dead
Sit down in groups and watch TV,
In which they must be interested,
For on it they see you and me.

These four, who though they never met
Died in one month, sit side by side
Together in front of the same set,
And all without a *TV Guide*.

Arms round each other's shoulders loosely,
Although they can feel nothing, who
When they unlearned their pain so sprucely
Let go of all sensation too.

Thus they watch friend and relative
And life here as they think it is
– In black and white, repetitive
As situation comedies.

With both delight and tears at first
They greet each programme on death's stations,
But in the end lose interest,
Their boredom turning to impatience.

   This remarkable book – so filled with life, so filled
with grief and death – ends remarkably and hope-
fully with a poem entitled "A Blank," in which, after
a wave of grief, the poet encounters, from a bus, a
former lover with a child he had adopted. The poem
begins:

The year of griefs being through, they had to merge
In one last grief, with one last property:
To view itself like loosened cloud lose edge,
And pull apart, and leave a voided sky.

And continues later:

. . . So this was his son!
What I admired about his self-permission
Was that he turned from nothing he had done,
Or was, or had been, even while he transposed
The expectations he took out at dark
– Of Eros playing, features undisclosed –
Into another pitch, where he might work
With the same melody, and opted so
To educate, permit, guide, feed, keep warm,
And love a child to be adopted, though
The child was still a blank then on a form.

The blank was flesh now, running on its nerve,
The fair-topped organism dense with charm,
Its braided muscle grabbing what would serve,
His countering pull, his own devoted arm.

This poem, the last in the book, makes a nice book-
end, I think, with the book's first poem, "The Hug." I
shouldn't imagine this was lost on Thom Gunn; not
much of interest ever was, in poetry or life.

AUGUST KLEINZAHLER was born in Jersey City in
1949. He is the author of ten books of poems and was
awarded the 2004 Griffin Poetry Prize for *The Strange
Hours Travelers Keep*. He lives in San Francisco.

I

The Hug

It was your birthday, we had drunk and dined
   Half of the night with our old friend
     Who'd showed us in the end
   To a bed I reached in one drunk stride.
     Already I lay snug,
And drowsy with the wine dozed on one side.

I dozed, I slept. My sleep broke on a hug,
     Suddenly, from behind,
In which the full lengths of our bodies pressed:
     Your instep to my heel,
   My shoulder-blades against your chest.
   It was not sex, but I could feel
   The whole strength of your body set,
     Or braced, to mine,
     And locking me to you
   As if we were still twenty-two
   When our grand passion had not yet
     Become familial.
   My quick sleep had deleted all
   Of intervening time and place.
     I only knew
The stay of your secure firm dry embrace.

To a Friend in Time of Trouble

You wake tired, in the cabin light has filled,
Then walk out to the deck you helped to build,
And pause, your senses reaching out anxiously,
Tentatively, toward scrub and giant tree:
A giving of the self instructed by
The dog who settles near you with a sigh
And seeks you in your movements, following each.
Though yours are different senses, they too reach
Until you know that they engage the air
— The clean and penetrable medium where
You encounter as if they were a sort of home
Fountains of fern that jet from the coarse loam.

You listen for the quiet, but hear instead
A sudden run of cries break overhead,
And look to see a wide-winged bird of prey
Between the redwood tops carrying away
Some small dark bundle outlined in its claws.
The certainty, the ease with which it draws
Its arc on blue . . . Soon the protesting shriek,
The gorging from the breast, the reddened beak,
The steadying claw withdrawn at last. You know
It is not cruel, it is not human, though
You cringe who would not feel surprised to find
Such lacerations made by mind on mind.

Later, the job, you haul large stones uphill.
You intend to pile them in a wall which will,
In front of plantings and good dirt, retain
Through many a winter of eroding rain.
Hard work and tiring, but the exercise
Opens the blood to air and simplifies
The memory of your troubles in the city,
Until you view them unconfused by pity.

A handsome grey-haired, grey-eyed man, tight-knit;
Each muscle clenching as you call on it
From the charmed empire of your middle age.
You move about your chores: the grief and rage
You brought out here begin at last to unbind.
And all day as you climb, the released mind
Unclenches till – the moment of release
Clean overlooked in the access of its own peace –
It finds that it has lost itself upon
The smooth red body of a young madrone,
From which it turns toward other varying shades
On the brown hillside where light grows and fades,
And feels the healing start, and still returns,
Riding its own repose, and learns, and learns.

Bone

It was at first your great
Halo of aureate-
brown curls distracted me.
And it was a distraction
Not from the hard-filled lean
Body that I desired
But from the true direction
Your face took, what it could mean,
Though it was there to see.

When you, that second day,
Drew back the shower curtain,
Another man stood there,
His drowned hair lay
Chastened and flattened down,
And I saw then for certain
How Blackfoot Indian bone
Persisting in the cheek,
The forehead, nape, and crown,
Had underlain the hair,
Which was mere ornament
– A European mock.

Could that be what it meant?
That high unsoftened rock
With no trees on.

An Invitation

from San Francisco
to my brother

Dear welcomer, I think you must agree
 It is your turn to visit me.
I'll put you in my room, sunk far from light,
 Where cars will not drive through your night.
Out of the window you can sneak a look
 To see some jolly neighbours cook
Down in their kitchen, like a lighted box
 Beyond the fence, where over fox-
glove, mint, and ribs of fern, the small dark plain
 Fingers of ivy graze my pane.
(Perhaps before you come I'll snip them off.)
 Once you have rested up enough
We'll bolt our porridge down before it's cool
 As if about to go to school.
But we are grown-up now, and we can go
 To watch the banked Pacific throw
Its rolling punches at a flowered hill
 Where garden seeds were dumped in fill.
Or we can take the Ferry across the Bay
 Scanning the washed views on our way
To Sausalito where the thing to do
 Is look at yet another view
And take the Ferry back. Or we can climb
 To murals from an earlier time:
A chunky proletariat of paint
 In allegorical restraint
Where fat silk-hatted bosses strut and cower

7

Around the walls inside a tower
Shaped like the nozzle of a fireman's hose.

By then you will have noticed those
Who make up Reagan's proletariat:
    The hungry in their long lines that
Gangling around two sides of city block
    Are fully formed by ten o'clock
For meals the good Franciscan fathers feed
    Without demur to all who need.
You'll watch the jobless side by side with whores
    Setting a home up out of doors.
And every day more crazies who debate
    With phantom enemies on the street.
I did see one with bright belligerent eye
    Gaze from a doorstep at the sky
And give the finger, with both hands, to God:
    But understand, he was not odd
Among the circumstances.
                    Well, I think
    After all that, we'll need a drink.
We may climb hills, but won't tax a beginner
    Just yet, and so come home to dinner
With my whole household, where they all excel:
    Each cooks one night, and each cooks well.
And while food lasts, and after it is gone,
    We'll talk, without a TV on,
We'll talk of all our luck and lack of luck,
    Of the foul job in which you're stuck,
Of friends, of the estranged and of the dead
    Or living relatives instead,
Of what we've done and seen and thought and read,
    Until we talk ourselves to bed.

The Differences

Reciting Adrienne Rich on Cole and Haight,
Your blond hair bouncing like a corner boy's,
You walked with sturdy almost swaggering gait,
The short man's, looking upward with such poise,
Such bold yet friendly curiosity
I was convinced that clear defiant blue
Would have abashed a storm-trooper. To me
Conscience and courage stood fleshed out in you.

So when you gnawed my armpits, I gnawed yours
And learned to associate you with that smell
As if your exuberance sprang from your pores.
I tried to lose my self in you as well.
To lose my self . . . I did the opposite,
I turned into the boy with iron teeth
Who planned to eat the whole world bit by bit,
My love not flesh but in the mind beneath.

Love takes its shape within that part of me
(A poet says) *where memories reside.*
And just as light marks out the boundary
Of some glass outline men can see inside,
So love is formed by a dark ray's invasion
From Mars, its dwelling in the mind to make.
Is a created thing, and has sensation,
A soul, and strength of will.
                                    It is opaque.

Opaque, yet once I slept with you all night
Dreaming about you – though not quite embraced
Always in contact felt however slight.
We lay at ease, an arm loose round a waist,
Or side by side and touching at the hips,
As if we were two trees, bough grazing bough,
The twigs being the toes or fingertips.
I have not crossed your mind for three weeks now,

But think back on that night in January,
When casually distinct we shared the most
And lay upon a bed of clarity
In luminous half-sleep where the will was lost.
We woke at times and as the night got colder
Exchanged a word, or pulled the clothes again
To cover up the other's exposed shoulder,
Falling asleep to the small talk of the rain.

Lines for My 55th Birthday

The love of old men is not worth a lot,
Desperate and dry even when it is hot.
You cannot tell what is enthusiasm
And what involuntary clawing spasm.

Philemon and Baucis

love without shadows – W.C.W.

Two trunks like bodies, bodies like twined trunks
Supported by their wooden hug. Leaves shine
In tender habit at the extremities.
Truly each other's, they have embraced so long
Their barks have met and wedded in one flow
Blanketing both. Time lights the handsome bulk.
  The gods were grateful, and for comfort given
Gave comfort multiplied a thousandfold.
Therefore the couple leached into that soil
The differences prolonged through their late vigour
That kept their exchanges salty and abrasive,
And found, with loves balancing equally,
Full peace of mind. They put unease behind them
A long time back, a long time back forgot
How each woke separate through the pale grey night,
A long time back forgot the days when each
– Riding the other's nervous exuberance –
Knew the slow thrill of learning how to love
What, gradually revealed, becomes itself,
Expands, unsheathes, as the keen rays explore:
Invented in the continuous revelation.

They have drifted into a perpetual nap,
The peace of trees that all night whisper nothings.

Odysseus on Hermes

his afterthought

I was seduced by innocence
– beard scarcely visible on his chin –
by the god within.
The incompletion of youth
like the new limb of the cactus growing
– soft-green – not fully formed
the spines still soft and living,
potent in potential,
in process and so
still open to the god.
        When complete and settled
        then closed to the god.
So sensing it in him
I was seduced by the god,
becoming in my thick maturity
suddenly unsettled
              un-solid
still being formed –
in the vulnerability, edges flowing,
myself open to the god.

I took his drug
and all came out right in the story.
Still thinking back
I seek to renew that power

so easily got
seek to find again that knack
of opening my settled features,
creased on themselves,
to the astonishing kiss and gift
of the wily god to the wily man.

Seesaw

song

Days are bright,
Nights are dark.
We play seesaw
In the park.

Look at me
And my friend
Freckleface
The other end.

Shiny board
Between my legs.
Feet crunch down
On the twigs.

I crouch close
To the ground
Till it's time:
Up I bound.

Legs go loose,
Legs go tight.
I drop down
Like the night.

Like a scales.
Give and take,
Take and give.
My legs ache.

So it ends
As it begins.
Off we climb
And no one wins.

2

A Sketch of the Great Dejection

Having read the promise of the hedgerow
the body set out anew on its adventures.
At length it came to a place of poverty,
of inner and outer famine,
                    where all movement had stopped
except for that of the wind, which was continual
and came from elsewhere, from the sea,
moving across unplanted fields and between headstones
in the little churchyard clogged with nettles
where no one came between Sundays, and few then.
The wind was like a punishment to the face and hands.
These were marshes of privation:
the mud of the ditches oozed scummy water,
the grey reeds were arrested in growth,
the sun did not show, even as a blur,
and the uneven lands were without definition
as I was without potent words,
inert.
                    I sat upon a disintegrating gravestone.
How can I continue, I asked?
I longed to whet my senses, but upon what?
On mud? It was a desert of raw mud.
I was tempted by fantasies of the past,
but my body rejected them, for only in the present
could it pursue the promise,
                    keeping open to its fulfilment.
I would not, either, sink into the mud,
warming it with the warmth I brought to it,
                    as in a sty of sloth.

19

My body insisted on restlessness
                having been promised love,
as my mind insisted on words
                having been promised the imagination.
So I remained alert, confused and uncomforted.
I fared on and, though the landscape did not change,
it came to seem after a while like a place of recuperation.

3

Patch Work

The bird book says, common, conspicuous.
This time of year all day
The mocking bird
Sweeps at a moderate height
Above the densely flowering
Suburban plots of May,
The characteristic shine
Of white patch cutting through the curved ash-grey
That bars each wing;
Or it appears to us
Perched on the post that ends a washing-line
To sing there, as in flight,
A repertoire of songs that it has heard
– From other birds, and others of its kind –
Which it has recombined
And made its own, especially one
With a few separate plangent notes begun
Then linking trills as a long confident run
Toward the immediate distance,
Repeated all day through
In the sexual longings of the spring
(Which also are derivative)
And almost mounting to
Fulfilment, thus to give
Such muscular vigour to a note so strong,
Fulfilment that does not destroy
The original, still-unspent
Longings that led it where it went
But links them in a bird's inhuman joy

Lifted upon the wing
Of that patched body, that insistence
Which fills the gardens up with headlong song.

The Life of the Otter

Tucson Desert Museum

From sand he pours himself into deep water,
His other liberty
                in which he swims
Faster than anything that lives on legs,
In wide parabolas
                figures of eight
Long loops
                drawn with the accuracy and ease
Of a lithe skater hands behind her back
Who seems to be showing off
                        but is half lost
In the exuberance of dip and wheel.

The small but long brown beast reaches from play
Through play
           to play
                play not as relaxation
Or practice or escape but all there is:
Activity   (hunt, procreation, feeding)
Functional but as if gratuitous.

Now
      while he flows
                    out of a downward curve
I glimpse through glass
                  his genitals as neat
As a stone acorn with its two oak leaves

25

Carved in a French cathedral porch,
                              relief
Exposed
          crisply detailed
                              above the sway
Of this firm muscular trunk
                              caught in mid-plunge,
Of which the speed contains its own repose
Potency
          set in fur
                    like an ornament.

Three for Children

Cannibal

Shark, with your mouth tucked under
That severs like a knife,
You leave no time for wonder
In your swift thrusting life.

You taste blood. It's your brother's,
And at your side he flits.
But blood, like any other's.
You bite him into bits.

The Aquarium

The dolphins play
Inside their pool all day
And through its bright blue water swing and wheel.
Though on display
They send out on their way
A song that we hear as a long light squeal.

But what they say
Is 'Oh the world is play!
Look at these men we have no cause to thank:
If only they
Would free themselves in play,
As we do even in this confining tank.'

The Seabed

A moray eel lies wound amongst the stone,
Colour of sand, its mouth a level slit.
Of all it snaps up here, and makes its own,
Octopus tentacles are its favourite.
It waits. Although it would not mean to hurt
A human if it met one in this spot,
It has indeed been known, although alert,
To make mistakes, as which of us has not.
For if across the underwater sand
Skindivers sometimes dancingly intrude,
It may confuse the fingers of a hand,
Wriggling through water, for its favourite food.

Skateboard

Tow Head on his skateboard
threads through a crowd
of feet and faces delayed
to a slow stupidity.
Darts, doubles, twists.
You notice how nimbly
the body itself has learned
to assess the relation between
the board, pedestrians,
and immediate sidewalk.
Emblem. Emblem of fashion.
Wearing dirty white
in dishevelment as delicate
as the falling draperies
on a dandyish
Renaissance saint.
Chain round his waist.
One hand gloved.
Hair dyed to show it is dyed,
pale flame spiking from fuel.
Tow Head on Skateboard
perfecting himself:
emblem extraordinary
of the ordinary.

In the sexless face
eyes innocent of feeling
therefore suggest the spirit.

Well Dennis O'Grady

Well Dennis O'Grady
said the smiling old woman
pausing at the bus stop I hear
they are still praying for you
I read it in the Bulletin.

His wattle throat sagged
above his careful tie and clean brown suit.
I didn't hear his answer,
but though bent a bit
over his stick
he was delighted to be out
in the slight December sunshine
– having a good walk, pleased
it seems at all the prayers
and walking pretty straight
on his own.

Outside the Diner

Off garbage outside the diner
he licks the different flavours
of greasy paper like a dog
and then unlike a dog
eats the paper too.

Times are
there's a lethargic
conviviality, as they sit around
a waste lot passing muscatel
which warms each in his sour sheath
worn so long that the smell
is complex, reminiscent
of food cooking or faeces.

Times are
there's the Detox Clinic, times are
he sleeps it off across the back seat
of an auto with four flat tyres,
blackened sole and heel
jammed against the side windows,
bearded face blinded by sleep
turned toward the light.
Another lies on the front seat.

A poor weed,
unwanted scraggle tufted
with unlovely yellow,
persists between paving stones
marginal to the grid
bearded face turned toward light.

Improvisation

I said our lives are improvisation and it sounded
un-rigid, liberal, in short a good idea.
But that kind of thing is hard to keep up:
guilty lest I gave to the good-looking only
I decided to hand him a quarter
whenever I saw him – what an ugly young man:
wide face, round cracked lips, big forehead
striped with greasy hairs. One day he said
'You always come through' and I do, I did,
except that time he was having a tantrum
hitting a woman, everyone moving away,
I pretending not to see, ashamed.
                                                    Mostly
he perches on the ungiving sidewalk, shits
behind bushes in the park, seldom weeps,
sleeps bandaged against the cold, curled
on himself like a wild creature,
his agility of mind wholly employed
with scrounging for cigarettes, drugs, drink
or the price of Ding Dongs, with dodging knife-fights,
with ducking cops and lunatics, his existence
paved with specifics like an Imagist epic,
the only discourse printed on shreds of newspaper,
not one of which carries the word improvisation.

Old Meg

dark as a gypsy, berry-
brown with dirt
sticks to the laundromats
in cold weather
             in the sun
sit near her on the bus-bench
and you'll smell something
of dog, something of mould

I've seen her beaming
at concrete 'You didn't make sense
at first I couldn't have known
who you were' Extraterrestrial
friends no doubt
             But to me
venturing once to greet her
she responded with
                'Blood on you!'

Yellow Pitcher Plant

flowering stomach

scroll of leaf

covered with small honeyed
warts by which the seely fly
is lured to sloping
pastures at the trumpet's lip

till grazing downhill
the fly finds the underbrush
of hairs casually pushed through
has closed behind —
a thicket of lances — sharkteeth —
trap
           oh alas!
it stumbles on, falling
from chamber to chamber
within the green turret
making each loud
with the buzz of its grief
and finally slipping into
the oubliette itself
— pool that digests protein —

to become mere
chitinous exoskeleton,
leftovers

of a sated petal

an enzyme's cruelty

Tenderloin

This poverty recognizes
a street only as link
between corners greasy
with expedient, corners
turned or waited on
slippery as they may be
for transactions, or news of them.

Not poverty beaten
down, poverty rather
on the make, without being
clever enough to make it.
Smallish sums pass hands.
This poverty seeks out
stereotype: gentle
black whore, foul-mouthed
old cripple, snarling skinhead,
tottering transvestite, etc.
City romantics.
Come on, you,
obey your impulse,
costs only a little more
than in the country.

It's all so
slippery, but
you might say one lubricant
is as good as another.

And there's no such thing
as an insincere
erection is there?

Think of Spanish
Fly, it irritates
the urethra which
has been capable, however,
of responding
to more delicate stimuli.

And of the loins too,
firm open slopes that lead
to the padded valley
Tender loin
protecting the serviceable
channel and glands
delicate almost as
eyeballs — Tender-
ness anaesthetized and irritated

Strip it bare

Grease it well
with its own foul
lubricant

Against the grit
of its own sharp corners
scrape it to orgasm

Looks

Those eyes appear to transmit energy
And hold it back undissipated too.
His gaze is like a star, that cannot see,
A glow so steady he directs at you
You try to be the first to look aside
— Less flattered by the appearance of attention
Than vexed by the dim stirrings thus implied
Within a mind kept largely in suspension.

Although a gaze sought out, and highly placed,
By lovers and photographers, it is
Too patly overwhelming for your taste.
You step back from such mannered solemnities
To focus on his no doubt sinewy power,
His restless movements, and his bony cheek.
You have seen him in the space of one half-hour
Cross a street twenty times. You have heard him speak,
Reading his work to the surprise of guests
Who find that dinner was a stratagem:
Poems in which the attracted turn to pests
If they touch him before he touches them,
In which the celebrant of an appetite
Richly fulfilled will say Get off me bitch
To one who thought she had an equal right
To her desires, — nevertheless in which
He holds you by the voice of his demands,
Which take unfaltering body on the air
As need itself, live, famished, clenched like hands
Pale at the knuckle. Then, his luminous stare,

That too. He is an actor, after all,
And it's a genuine talent he engages
In playing this one character, mean, small,
But driven like Othello by his rages
As if a passion for no matter what,
Even the self, is fully justified,
Or as if anger could repopulate
The bony city he is trapped inside.

At times he has a lover he can hurt
By bringing home the pick-ups he despises
Because they let him pick them up. Alert
Always to looks – and they must look like prizes –
He blurs further distinction, for he knows
Nothing of strength but its apparent drift,
Tending and tending, and nothing of repose
Except within his kindled gaze, his gift.

To Isherwood Dying

It could be, Christopher, from your leafed-in house
In Santa Monica where you lie and wait
   You hear outside a sound resume
     Fitful, anonymous,
   Of Berlin fifty years ago
   As autumn days got late –
The whistling to their girls from young men who
   Stood in the deep dim street, below
Dingy façades which crumbled like a cliff,
   Behind which in a rented room
     You listened, wondering if
By chance one might be whistling up for you,
   Adding unsentimentally
     'It could not possibly be.'
Now it's a stricter vigil that you hold
And from the canyon's palms and crumbled gold
   It could be possibly
   You hear a single whistle call
     Come out
   Come out into the cold.
Courting insistent and impersonal.

                      Christmas week, 1985

The Stealer

I lie and live
my body's fear
something's at large
and coming near

No deadbolt
can keep it back
A worm of fog
leaks through a crack

From the darkness
as before
it grows to body
in my door

Like a taker
scarved and gloved
it steals this way
like one I loved

Fear stiffens me
and a slow joy
at the approach
of the sheathed boy

Will he too do
what that one did
unlock me first
open the lid

and reach inside
with playful feel
all the better
thus to steal

JVC

He concentrated, as he ought,
On fitting language to his thought
And getting all the rhymes correct,
Thus exercising intellect
In such a space, in such a fashion,
He concentrated into passion.

Barren Leaves

Spontaneous overflows of powerful feeling:
Wet dreams, wet dreams, in libraries congealing.

Jamesian

Their relationship consisted
In discussing if it existed.

Meat

My brother saw a pig root in a field,
And saw too its whole lovely body yield
To this desire which deepened out of need
So that in wriggling through the mud and weed
To eat and dig were one athletic joy.
When we who are the overlords destroy
Our ranging vassals, we can therefore taste
The muscle of delighted interest
We make into ourselves, as formerly
Hurons digested human bravery.

Not much like this degraded meat – this meal
Of something, was it chicken, pork, or veal?
It tasted of the half-life that we raise
In high bright tombs which, days, and nights like days,
Murmur with nervous sound from cubicles
Where fed on treated slop the living cells
Expand within each creature forced to sit
Cramped with its boredom and its pile of shit
Till it is standard weight for roast or bacon
And terminated, and its place is taken.

To make this worth a meal you have to add
The succulent liberties it never had
Of leek, or pepper fruiting in its climb,
The redolent adventures dried in thyme
Whose branches creep and stiffen where they please,
Or rosemary that shakes in the world's breeze.

47

Cafeteria in Boston

I could digest the white slick watery mash,
The two green peppers stuffed with rice and grease
In Harry's Cafeteria, could digest
Angelfood cake too like a sweetened sawdust.
I sought to extend the body's education,
Forced it to swallow down the blunted dazzle
Sucked from the red formica where I leaned.
Took myself farther, digesting as I went,
Course after course: even the bloated man
In cast-off janitor's overalls, who may
Indeed have strayed through only for the toilets;
But as he left I caught his hang-dog stare
At the abandoned platefuls crusted stiff
Like poisoned slugs that froth into their trails.
I stomached him, him of the flabby stomach,
Though it was getting harder to keep down.
But how about the creature scurrying in
From the crowds wet on the November sidewalk,
His face a black skull with a slaty shine,
Who slipped his body with one fluid motion
Into a seat before a dish on which
Scrapings had built a heterogeneous mound,
And set about transferring them to his mouth,
Stacking them faster there than he could swallow,
To get a start on the bus-boys. My mouth too
Was packed, its tastes confused: what bitter juices
I generated in my stomach as
Revulsion met revulsion. Yet at last
I lighted upon meat more to my taste

When, glancing off into the wide fluorescence,
I saw the register, where the owner sat,
And suddenly realized that he, the cooks,
The servers of the line, the bus-boys, all
Kept their eyes studiously turned away
From the black scavenger. Digestively,
That was the course that kept the others down.

Nasturtium

Born in a sour waste lot
You laboured up to light,
Bunching what strength you'd got
And running out of sight
Through a knot-hole at last,
To come forth into sun
As if without a past,
Done with it, re-begun.

Now street-side of the fence
You take a few green turns,
Nimble in nonchalance
Before your first flower burns.
From poverty and prison
And undernourishment
A prodigal has risen,
Self-spending, never spent.

Irregular yellow shell
And drooping spur behind . . .
Not rare but beautiful
– Street-handsome – as you wind
And leap, hold after hold,
A golden runaway
Still running, strewing gold
From side to side all day.

The Beautician

She, a beautician, came to see her friend
Inside the morgue, when she had had her cry.
She found the body dumped there all awry,
Not as she thought right for a person's end,
Left sideways like that on one arm and thigh.

In their familiarity with the dead
It was as if the men had not been kind
With her old friend, whose hair she was assigned
To fix and shape. She did not speak; instead
She gave her task a concentrated mind.

She did find in it some thin satisfaction
That she could use her tenderness as skill
To make her poor dead friend's hair beautiful
– As if she shaped an epitaph by her action,
She thought – being a beautician after all.

'All Do Not All Things Well'

Implies that some therefore
Do well, for its own sake,
One thing they undertake,
Because it has enthralled them.

I used to like the two
Auto freaks as I called them
Who laboured in their driveway,
Its concrete black with oil,
In the next block that year.

One, hurt in jungle war,
Had a false leg, the other
Raised a huge beard above
A huge Hell's Angel belly.

They seemed to live on beer
And corn chips from the deli.

Always with friends, they sprawled
Beneath a ruined car
In that inert but live way
Of scrutinizing innards.
And one week they extracted
An engine to examine,
Transplant shining like tar
Fished out into the sun.

'It's all that I enjoy,'
Said the stiff-legged boy.
That was when the officious
Realtor had threatened them
For brashly operating
A business on the street
— An outsider, that woman
Who wanted them evicted,
Wanted the neighbourhood neat
To sell it. That was when
The boy from Viet Nam told me
That he'd firebomb her car.
He didn't of course, she won.

I am sorry that they went.
Quick with a friendly greeting,
They were gentle joky men
— Certainly not ambitious,
Perhaps not intelligent
Unless about a car,
Their work one thing they knew
They could for certain do
With a disinterest
And passionate expertise
To which they gave their best
Desires and energies.
Such oily-handed zest
By-passed the self like love.
I thought that they were good
For any neighbourhood.

4

Rain punishes the city,
like raw mind that batters flesh,
ever saddened by what fails.

Charlie Hinkle

The Man with Night Sweats

I wake up cold, I who
Prospered through dreams of heat
Wake to their residue,
Sweat, and a clinging sheet.

My flesh was its own shield:
Where it was gashed, it healed.

I grew as I explored
The body I could trust
Even while I adored
The risk that made robust,

A world of wonders in
Each challenge to the skin.

I cannot but be sorry
The given shield was cracked,
My mind reduced to hurry,
My flesh reduced and wrecked.

I have to change the bed,
But catch myself instead

Stopped upright where I am
Hugging my body to me
As if to shield it from
The pains that will go through me,

As if hands were enough
To hold an avalanche off.

In Time of Plague

My thoughts are crowded with death
and it draws so oddly on the sexual
that I am confused
confused to be attracted
by, in effect, my own annihilation.
Who are these two, these fiercely attractive men
who want me to stick their needle in my arm?
They tell me they are called Brad and John,
one from here, one from Denver, sitting the same
on the bench as they talk to me,
their legs spread apart, their eyes attentive.
I love their daring, their looks, their jargon,
and what they have in mind.

Their mind is the mind of death.
They know it, and do not know it,
and they are like me in that
(I know it, and do not know it)
and like the flow of people through this bar.
Brad and John thirst heroically together
for euphoria – for a state of ardent life
in which we could all stretch ourselves
and lose our differences. I seek
to enter their minds: am I a fool,
and they direct and right, properly
testing themselves against risk,
as a human must, and does,
or are they the fools, their alert faces
mere death's heads lighted glamorously?

I weigh possibilities
till I am afraid of the strength
of my own health
and of their evident health.

They get restless at last with my indecisiveness
and so, first one, and then the other,
move off into the moving concourse of people
who are boisterous and bright
carrying in their faces and throughout their bodies
the news of life and death.

Lament

Your dying was a difficult enterprise.
First, petty things took up your energies,
The small but clustering duties of the sick,
Irritant as the cough's dry rhetoric.
Those hours of waiting for pills, shot, X-ray
Or test (while you read novels two a day)
Already with a kind of clumsy stealth
Distanced you from the habits of your health.
   In hope still, courteous still, but tired and thin,
You tried to stay the man that you had been,
Treating each symptom as a mere mishap
Without import. But then the spinal tap.
It brought a hard headache, and when night came
I heard you wake up from the same bad dream
Every half-hour with the same short cry
Of mild outrage, before immediately
Slipping into the nightmare once again
Empty of content but the drip of pain.
No respite followed: though the nightmare ceased,
Your cough grew thick and rich, its strength increased.
Four nights, and on the fifth we drove you down
To the Emergency Room. That frown, that frown:
I'd never seen such rage in you before
As when they wheeled you through the swinging door.
For you knew, rightly, they conveyed you from
Those normal pleasures of the sun's kingdom
The hedonistic body basks within
And takes for granted – summer on the skin,
Sleep without break, the moderate taste of tea

In a dry mouth. You had gone on from me
As if your body sought out martyrdom
In the far Canada of a hospital room.
Once there, you entered fully the distress
And long pale rigours of the wilderness.
A gust of morphine hid you. Back in sight
You breathed through a segmented tube, fat, white,
Jammed down your throat so that you could not speak.
    How thin the distance made you. In your cheek
One day, appeared the true shape of your bone
No longer padded. Still your mind, alone,
Explored this emptying intermediate
State for what holds and rests were hidden in it.
    You wrote us messages on a pad, amused
At one time that you had your nurse confused
Who, seeing you reconciled after four years
With your grey father, both of you in tears,
Asked if this was at last your 'special friend'
(The one you waited for until the end).
'She sings,' you wrote, 'a Philippine folk song
To wake me in the morning . . . It is long
And very pretty.' Grabbing at detail
To furnish this bare ledge toured by the gale,
On which you lay, bed restful as a knife,
You tried, tried hard, to make of it a life
Thick with the complicating circumstance
Your thoughts might fasten on. It had been chance
Always till now that had filled up the moment
With live specifics your hilarious comment
Discovered as it went along; and fed,
Laconic, quick, wherever it was led.
You improvised upon your own delight.
I think back to the scented summer night

We talked between our sleeping bags, below
A molten field of stars five years ago:
I was so tickled by your mind's light touch
I couldn't sleep, you made me laugh too much,
Though I was tired and begged you to leave off.

Now you were tired, and yet not tired enough
– Still hungry for the great world you were losing
Steadily in no season of your choosing –
And when at last the whole death was assured,
Drugs having failed, and when you had endured
Two weeks of an abominable constraint,
You faced it equably, without complaint,
Unwhimpering, but not at peace with it.
You'd lived as if your time was infinite:
You were not ready and not reconciled,
Feeling as uncompleted as a child
Till you had shown the world what you could do
In some ambitious role to be worked through,
A role your need for it had half-defined,
But never wholly, even in your mind.
You lacked the necessary ruthlessness,
The soaring meanness that pinpoints success.
We loved that lack of self-love, and your smile,
Rueful, at your own silliness.
                                    Meanwhile,
Your lungs collapsed, and the machine, unstrained,
Did all your breathing now. Nothing remained
But death by drowning on an inland sea
Of your own fluids, which it seemed could be
Kindly forestalled by drugs. Both could and would:
Nothing was said, everything understood,
At least by us. Your own concerns were not

Long-term, precisely, when they gave the shot
– You made local arrangements to the bed
And pulled a pillow round beside your head.
    And so you slept, and died, your skin gone grey,
Achieving your completeness, in a way.

Outdoors next day, I was dizzy from a sense
Of being ejected with some violence
From vigil in a white and distant spot
Where I was numb, into this garden plot
Too warm, too close, and not enough like pain.
I was delivered into time again
– The variations that I live among
Where your long body too used to belong
And where the still bush is minutely active.
You never thought your body was attractive,
Though others did, and yet you trusted it
And must have loved its fickleness a bit
Since it was yours and gave you what it could,
Till near the end it let you down for good,
Its blood hospitable to those guests who
Took over by betraying it into
The greatest of its inconsistencies
This difficult, tedious, painful enterprise.

Terminal

The eight years difference in age seems now
Disparity so wide between the two
That when I see the man who armoured stood
Resistant to all help however good
Now helped through day itself, eased into chairs,
Or else led step by step down the long stairs
With firm and gentle guidance by his friend,
Who loves him, through each effort to descend,
Each wavering, each attempt made to complete
An arc of movement and bring down the feet
As if with that spare strength he used to enjoy,
I think of Oedipus, old, led by a boy.

Still Life

I shall not soon forget
The greyish-yellow skin
To which the face had set:
Lids tight: nothing of his,
No tremor from within,
Played on the surfaces.

He still found breath, and yet
It was an obscure knack.
I shall not soon forget
The angle of his head,
Arrested and reared back
On the crisp field of bed,

Back from what he could neither
Accept, as one opposed,
Nor, as a life-long breather,
Consentingly let go,
The tube his mouth enclosed
In an astonished O.

The Reassurance

About ten days or so
After we saw you dead
You came back in a dream.
I'm all right now you said.

And it *was* you, although
You were fleshed out again:
You hugged us all round then,
And gave your welcoming beam.

How like you to be kind,
Seeking to reassure.
And, yes, how like my mind
To make itself secure.

Words for Some Ash

Poor parched man, we had to squeeze
Dental sponge against your teeth,
So that moisture by degrees
Dribbled to the mouth beneath.

Christmas Day your pupils crossed,
Staring at your nose's tip,
Seeking there the air you lost
Yet still gaped for, dry of lip.

Now you are a bag of ash
Scattered on a coastal ridge,
Where you watched the distant crash,
Ocean on a broken edge.

Death has wiped away each sense;
Fire took muscle, bone, and brains;
Next may rain leach discontents
From your dust, wash what remains

Deeper into damper ground
Till the granules work their way
Down to unseen streams, and bound
Briskly in the water's play;

May you lastly reach the shore,
Joining tide without intent,
Only worried any more
By the currents' argument.

Sacred Heart

For one who watches with too little rest
A body rousing fitfully to its pain
— The nerves like dull burns where the sheet has pressed —
Subsiding to dementia yet again;
For one who snatches what repose he can,
Exhausted by the fretful reflexes
Jerked from the torpor of a dying man,
Sleep is a fear, invaded as it is
By coil on coil of ominous narrative
In which specific isolated streaks,
Bright as tattoos, of inks that seem to live,
Shift through elusive patterns. Once in those weeks
You dreamt your dying friend hung crucified
In his front room, against the mantelpiece;
Yet it was Christmas, when you went outside
The shoppers bustled, bells rang without cease,
You smelt a sharp excitement on the air,
Crude itch of evergreen. But you returned
To find him still nailed up, mute sufferer
Lost in a trance of pain, toward whom you yearned.
When you woke up, you could not reconcile
The two conflicting scenes, indoors and out.
But it was Christmas. And parochial school
Accounted for the Dying God no doubt.

Now since his death you've lost the wish for sleep,
In which you might mislay the wound of feeling:

Drugged you drag grief from room to room and weep,
Preserving it from closure, from a healing
Into the novelty of glazed pink flesh.
We hear you stumble vision-ward above,
Keeping the edges open, bloody, fresh.

Wound, no – the heart, His Heart, broken with love.

An unfamiliar ticking makes you look
Down your left side where, suddenly apparent
Like a bright plate from an anatomy book
– In its snug housing, under the transparent
Planes of swept muscle and the barrelled bone –
The heart glows, and you feel the holy heat:
The heart of hearts transplanted to your own
Losing rich purple drops with every beat.
Yet even as it does your vision alters,
The hallucination lighted through the skin
Begins to deaden (though still bleeding), falters,
And hardens to its evident origin
– A red heart from a cheap religious card,
Too smooth, too glossy, too securely cased!

Stopped in a crouch, you wearily regard
Each drop dilute into the waiting waste.

Her Pet

I walk the floor, read, watch a cop-show, drink,
Hear buses heave uphill through drizzling fog,
Then turn back to the pictured book to think
Of Valentine Balbiani and her dog:
She is reclining, reading, on her tomb;
But pounced, it tries to intercept her look,
Its front paws on her lap, as in this room
The cat attempts to nose beneath my book.

Her curls tight, breasts held by her bodice high,
Ruff crisp, mouth calm, hands long and delicate,
All in the pause of marble signify
A strength so lavish she can limit it.
She will not let her pet dog catch her eye
For dignity, and for a touch of wit.

Below, from the same tomb, is reproduced
A side-relief, in which she reappears
Without her dog, and everything is loosed –
Her hair down from the secret of her ears,
Her big ears, and her creased face genderless
Craning from sinewy throat. Death is so plain!
Her breasts are low knobs through the unbound dress.
In the worked features I can read the pain
She went through to get here, to shake it all,
Thinking at first that her full nimble strength
Hid like a little dog within recall,

Till to think so, she knew, was to pretend
And, hope dismissed, she sought out pain at length
And laboured with it to bring on its end.

The tomb is by Germain Pilon. It is illustrated in Michael Levey's *High Renaissance* (Penguin Books), p. 129.

Courtesies of the Interregnum

a memory of the Colonnades, Sept. 1986

He speaks of eating three hot meals a day
To bolster off the absence on its way.
In Juárez, too, a medicine is sold
That holds the immune cells firm, he has been told.
Expert of health, he watches every trend.
It truly must be difficult for my friend
To hold on to the substance that is him,
Once sternly regulated in the gym,
Prime flesh now softening on his giant frame.

When he gave weekly dinners here, we came
To this large white room with white furnishings,
Where in dim patience among handsome things
He awaits the day's event now – the late sun
At regular exercise, its daily run
Across the polished floorboards, tamed, discreet,
That swaggered over shoulders in the street.

Yet even while subdued to his pale room,
He rallies, smiles, I see he has become
The man I know – for suddenly aware
That he forgot his guest in his despair,
He is, confronted by a guest so fit,
Almost concerned lest I feel out of it,
Excluded from the invitation list
To the largest gathering of the decade, missed
From membership as if the club were full.
It is not that I am not eligible,

73

He gallantly implies. *He* is, for sure
– The athlete to be asked out one time more.
And he now, athlete-like, triumphs at length,
Though with not physical but social strength
Precisely exerted. He who might well cry
Reaches through such informal courtesy
To values grasped and shaped out as he goes,
Of which the last is bravery, for he knows
That even as he gets them in his grip
Context itself starts dizzyingly to slip.

To the Dead Owner of a Gym

I will remember well
The elegant decision
To that red line of tile
As margin round the showers
Of your gym, Norm,
In which so dashing a physique
As yours for several years
Gained muscle every week
With sharper definition.
Death on the other hand
Is rigid and,
Finally as it may define
An absence with its cutting line,
     Alas,
     Lacks class.

Memory Unsettled

Your pain still hangs in air,
Sharp motes of it suspended;
The voice of your despair –
That also is not ended:

When near your death a friend
Asked you what he could do,
'Remember me,' you said.
We will remember you.

Once when you went to see
Another with a fever
In a like hospital bed,
With terrible hothouse cough
And terrible hothouse shiver
That soaked him and then dried him,
And you perceived that he
Had to be comforted,

You climbed in there beside him
And hugged him plain in view,
Though you were sick enough,
And had your own fears too.

The J Car

Last year I used to ride the J CHURCH Line,
Climbing between small yards recessed with vine
– Their ordered privacy, their plots of flowers
Like blameless lives we might imagine ours.
Most trees were cut back, but some brushed the car
Before it swung round to the street once more
On which I rolled out almost to the end,
To 29th Street, calling for my friend.
  He'd be there at the door, smiling but gaunt,
To set out for the German restaurant.
There, since his sight was tattered now, I would
First read the menu out. He liked the food
In which a sourness and dark richness meet
For conflict without taste of a defeat,
As in the Sauerbraten. What he ate
I hoped would help him to put on some weight,
But though the crusted pancakes might attract
They did so more as concept than in fact,
And I'd eat his dessert before we both
Rose from the neat arrangement of the cloth,
Where the connection between life and food
Had briefly seemed so obvious if so crude.
Our conversation circumspectly cheerful,
We had sat here like children good but fearful
Who think if they behave everything might
Still against likelihood come out all right.
  But it would not, and we could not stay here:
Finishing up the Optimator beer

I walked him home through the suburban cool
By dimming shape of church and Catholic school,
Only a few white teenagers about.
After the four blocks he would be tired out.
I'd leave him to the feverish sleep ahead,
Myself to ride through darkened yards instead
Back to my health. Of course I simplify.
Of course. It tears me still that he should die
As only an apprentice to his trade,
The ultimate engagements not yet made.
His gifts had been withdrawing one by one
Even before their usefulness was done:
This optic nerve would never be relit;
The other flickered, soon to be with it.
Unready, disappointed, unachieved,
He knew he would not write the much-conceived
Much-hoped-for work now, nor yet help create
A love he might in full reciprocate.

To a Dead Graduate Student

The whole rich process of twined opposites,
Tendril round stalk, developing in tandem
Through tangled exquisite detail that knits
To a unique promise –
                      checked at random,
Killed, wasted. What a teacher you'd have made:
Your tough impatient mind, your flowering looks
Would have seduced the backward where they played,
Rebels like you, to share your love of books.

The Missing

Now as I watch the progress of the plague,
The friends surrounding me fall sick, grow thin,
And drop away. Bared, is my shape less vague
– Sharply exposed and with a sculpted skin?

I do not like the statue's chill contour,
Not nowadays. The warmth investing me
Led outward through mind, limb, feeling, and more
In an involved increasing family.

Contact of friend led to another friend,
Supple entwinement through the living mass
Which for all that I knew might have no end,
Image of an unlimited embrace.

I did not just feel ease, though comfortable:
Aggressive as in some ideal of sport,
With ceaseless movement thrilling through the whole,
Their push kept me as firm as their support.

But death – Their deaths have left me less defined:
It was their pulsing presence made me clear.
I borrowed from it, I was unconfined,
Who tonight balance unsupported here,

Eyes glaring from raw marble, in a pose
Languorously part-buried in the block,
Shins perfect and no calves, as if I froze
Between potential and a finished work.

– Abandoned incomplete, shape of a shape,
In which exact detail shows the more strange,
Trapped in unwholeness, I find no escape
Back to the play of constant give and change.

August 1987

Death's Door

Of course the dead outnumber us
– How their recruiting armies grow!
My mother archaic now as Minos,
She who died forty years ago.

After their processing, the dead
Sit down in groups and watch TV,
In which they must be interested,
For on it they see you and me.

These four, who though they never met
Died in one month, sit side by side
Together in front of the same set,
And all without a *TV Guide.*

Arms round each other's shoulders loosely,
Although they can feel nothing, who
When they unlearned their pain so sprucely
Let go of all sensation too.

Thus they watch friend and relative
And life here as they think it is
– In black and white, repetitive
As situation comedies.

With both delight and tears at first
They greet each programme on death's stations,
But in the end lose interest,
Their boredom turning to impatience.

'He misses me? He must be kidding
— This week he's sleeping with a cop.'
'All she reads now is *Little Gidding*.'
'They're getting old. I wish they'd stop.'

The habit of companionship
Lapses — they break themselves of touch:
Edging apart at arm and hip,
Till separated on the couch,

They woo amnesia, look away
As if they were not yet elsewhere,
And when snow blurs the picture they,
Turned, give it a belonging stare.

Snow blows out toward them, till their seat
Filling with flakes becomes instead
Snow-bank, snow-landscape, and in that
They find themselves with all the dead,

Where passive light from snow-crust shows them
Both Minos circling and my mother.
Yet none of the recruits now knows them,
Nor do they recognize each other,

They have been so superbly trained
Into the perfect discipline
Of an archaic host, and weaned
From memory briefly barracked in.

A Blank

The year of griefs being through, they had to merge
In one last grief, with one last property:
To view itself like loosened cloud lose edge,
And pull apart, and leave a voided sky.

Watching Victorian porches through the glass,
From the 6 bus, I caught sight of a friend
Stopped on a corner-kerb to let us pass,
A four-year-old blond child tugging his hand,
Which tug he held against with a slight smile.
I knew the smile from certain passages
Two years ago, thus did not know him well,
Since they took place in my bedroom and his.

A sturdy-looking admirable young man.
He said 'I chose to do this with my life.'
Casually met he said it of the plan
He undertook without a friend or wife.

Now visibly tugged upon by his decision,
Wayward and eager. So this was his son!
What I admired about his self-permission
Was that he turned from nothing he had done,
Or was, or had been, even while he transposed
The expectations he took out at dark
— Of Eros playing, features undisclosed —
Into another pitch, where he might work

With the same melody, and opted so
To educate, permit, guide, feed, keep warm,
And love a child to be adopted, though
The child was still a blank then on a form.

The blank was flesh now, running on its nerve,
This fair-topped organism dense with charm,
Its braided muscle grabbing what would serve,
His countering pull, his own devoted arm.

Acknowledgements and Notes

Grateful acknowledgements are made to the editors and
publishers of the following periodicals, where the poems in this
book first appeared: *Agni, Berkeley Poetry Review, Chicago
Review, Contact II, Critical Quarterly, Gay Times, London
Review of Books, Numbers, Occident, Paris Review,
Ploughshares* ('The Beautician'), *PN Review, Poetry, Sagetrieb,
Scripsi, Sequoia, Sulfur, Threepenny Review, Tikkun, Times
Literary Supplement, Verse, Very Green, Yale Review,
ZYZZYVA.*

Some poems first appeared in the following pamphlets or
limited editions: *Sidewalks* (illustrated by Bill Schuessler,
Albondocani Press), *The Hurtless Trees* (illustrated by Andrew
Hudson, Jordan Davies), *Night Sweats* (Robert L. Barth),
Undesirables (Pig Press) and *Death's Door* (Red Hydra).
'Lament', which first appeared in the *London Review of
Books*, was printed as a pamphlet by Doe Press, illustrated by
Bill Schuessler. 'Skateboard' first appeared in a flyer published
by Off the Wall Gallery. 'Well Dennis O'Grady', which first
appeared in *Occident*, was later a bus-poster published by
Streetlines. 'Yellow Pitcher Plant' first appeared in *The Temple
of Flora* (Arion Press), two of the 'Three for Children' in *Birds,
Beasts and Fishes* (ed. Samuel Carr, Batsford) and 'Seesaw' in
Poetry World I (ed. Geoffrey Summerfield, Bell and Hyman).

The poet referred to in 'The Differences' is Guido Cavalcanti.
Some of the poems in this book refer to friends who died
before their time. For the record – for *my* record if for no one
else's, because they were not famous people – I wish to name
them here: 'The Reassurance' and 'Lament' are about Allan

Noseworthy; 'Terminal' and 'Words for Some Ash', Jim Lay; 'Still Life', Larry Hoyt; 'To the Dead Owner of a Gym' and 'Courtesies of the Interregnum', Norm Rathweg; 'Memory Unsettled', 'To a Dead Graduate Student' and 'The J Car', Charlie Hinkle, lines from whose *Poems* are quoted as an epigraph to Part 4. Two more, Lonnie Leard and Allen Day, enter less directly into other poems.

9 780374 530686